ORIGAMI TOYS

Florence Temko

Illustrations by Barbara Poeter
Based on original diagrams by Florence Temko

Photos by Dave Kutchukian

TUTTLE PUBLISHING
Boston • Rutland, Vermont • Tokyo

First published in the United States in 2003 by Tuttle Publishing, an imprint of Periplus Editions (HK) Ltd., with editorial offices at 153 Milk Street, Boston, Massachusetts 02109.

Library of Congress Cataloging-in-Publication Data

Temko, Florence
Origami toys / Florence Temko. – 1st ed.
   p. cm.
ISBN 0-8048-3478-4 (pbk.)
1. Origami. 2. Paper toy making. 3. Paper toys. I. Title

TT870 .T4467 2003
736'.982 – dc21   2002075058

Distributed by

North America, Latin America, and Europe
Tuttle Publishing
Distribution Center
Airport Industrial Park
364 Innovation Drive
North Clarendon, VT 05759-9436
Tel: (802) 773-8930
Fax: (802) 773-6993
Email: info@tuttlepublishing.com

Japan
Tuttle Publishing
Yaekari Building, 3F
5-4-12 Ōsaki, Shinagawa-ku
Tokyo 141-0032
Tel: 81-35-437-0171
Fax: 81-35-437-0755
Email: tuttle-sales@gol.com

Asia Pacific
Berkeley Books Pte. Ltd.
130 Joo Seng Road
#06-01/03 Olivine Building
Singapore 368357
Tel: (65) 6280-3320
Fax: (65) 6280-6290
Email: inquiries@periplus.com.sg

First edition
08 07 06 05 04 03   9 8 7 6 5 4 3 2 1

Design by Barbara Poeter, Bomoseen, Vermont
Printed in Singapore

CONTENTS

◣ Introduction

Origami Toys shows you how to make many paper toys and games that are fun for both children and adults. If you have ever folded a paper airplane you have already tried origami. Origami is the craft of folding a piece of paper into a recognizable object, using only your hands, which is exactly how you made the airplane. Many people are fascinated with origami and find it to be a relaxing, yet challenging hobby.

Origami Toys contains a lot of practical information, including:

- Step-by-step instructions
- How to make unique decorations
- How to create new designs
- How to use different papers
- How to teach origami
- How to use origami as an educational tool
- How origami fits into the world of computers and technology

You may be amazed at what's in store for you in *Origami Toys*.

◣ About Origami Techniques

To help you make sense of the lines and arrows on the drawings, you should study the explanations of a few basic techniques. It will be well worth a few minutes to learn to recognize the "Four Important Symbols" and "Three Procedures," which are international standards for origami.

Any action to be taken at each step is shown in red on the diagrams.

FOUR IMPORTANT SYMBOLS

Learn to recognize these four simple clues, which are often overlooked by beginners.

1. Valley Fold

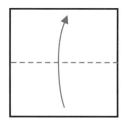

Fold the square in half by bringing one edge of the paper toward you and matching it to the opposite edge.

A valley fold is always shown by a line of dashes. You have made a valley fold.

With this one simple fold, you have made a greeting card.

2. Mountain Fold

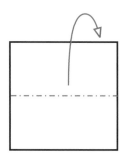

Fold the square in half by guiding one edge of the paper to the back and matching it to the opposite edge. A mountain fold is shown by a dash-dot-dash line and an arrow.

You have made a mountain fold.

With this one simple fold you have made a tent.

3. Arrows

Make a valley fold.

Double arrow — Fold and unfold.

Make a mountain fold.

Curly arrow — Turn the paper over.

4. Existing Crease

An existing crease, made previously, is shown by a thin line that does not touch the edges.

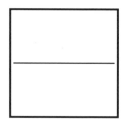

Existing crease

THREE PROCEDURES

In these three procedures, which occur frequently in paperfolding, several steps are combined into one standard process.

1. Inside Reverse Fold

One of the most common procedures is called an inside reverse fold.

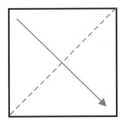 1. Fold a small square from corner to corner.

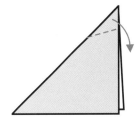 2. Place the paper exactly as shown. Fold the top corner over to the right, so that it peeks over the open edge.

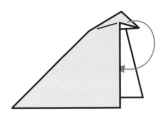 3a. Let the paper open up, and push the corner in between the two layers of paper, on the creases you made in Step 2.

3b. Close up the paper.

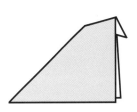 4. Completed inside reverse fold

The instructions for making an inside reverse fold are indicated with a dash-dot-dash line, the same as for a mountain fold, but the text states that you must make an inside reverse fold.

You may wonder why this procedure is called a reverse fold: In Step 2 you will see that the doubled paper is made up of a mountain fold on the front layer and a valley fold on the back layer. After you have pushed the corner in between the two layers of paper in Step 3, you have "reversed" the valley fold into a mountain fold.

2. Outside Reverse Fold

With an outside reverse fold, the paper is wrapped around the outside of a corner.

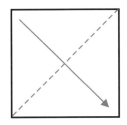 1. Fold a small square from corner to corner.

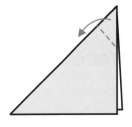 2. Place the paper exactly as shown. Valley fold the top corner over to the left, so that it peeks over the folded edge.

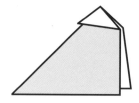

3a. Unfold Step 2.

3b. Let the paper open up and valley fold on the creases made in Step 2.

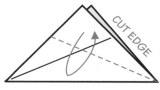

4. Completed outside reverse fold

Outside reverse folds are often used for heads, feet, and hats. The instructions for making an outside reverse fold are indicated with a dashed line, the same as for a valley fold, but the text states that you must make an outside reverse fold.

3. Rabbit's Ear

A rabbit's ear is always formed on a triangle, whenever it occurs during the folding of a model.

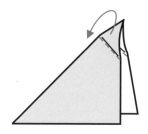

1. Fold a square from corner to corner.

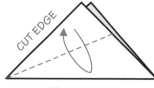

2. You now have a triangle. Fold one of the shorter cut edges to the long folded edge. Unfold it.

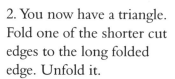

3. Fold the other short cut edge to the long folded edge. Unfold it.

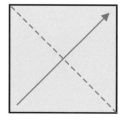

4. Pinch the corner between your thumb and forefinger so that it forms a valley fold that ends where the two creases made in Step 2 and Step 3 meet. The corner will stand up like a rabbit's ear.

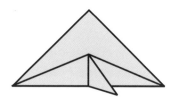

5. Completed Rabbit's Ear

HOW TO CUT PAPER SQUARES

Many of the projects in this book begin with a square piece of paper. All its sides are of equal length and all corners are right (90-degree) angles. Paper can be squared on a board paper cutter, if available, but it's quite easy to cut any rectangular sheet into a square:

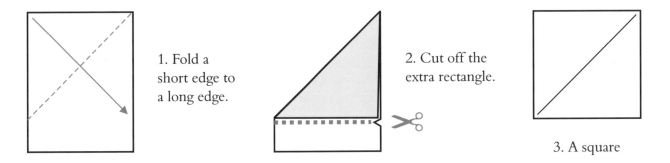

1. Fold a short edge to a long edge.

2. Cut off the extra rectangle.

3. A square

Sheets of 8 ½" x 11" copy and other printing papers can be cut into two sizes:

- With one cut: into squares with 8 ½" sides.
- With two cuts: into two squares with 5 ½" sides.

Copy shops will usually cut a whole ream for a small fee. A ream will provide five hundred 8 ½" squares or a thousand 5 ½" squares.

HELPFUL TIPS

If you are having trouble with a step check the following:

1. Make sure you distinguish carefully between a valley fold (dashed line) and a mountain fold (dash-dot-dash line).

2. Be sure to observe the curly arrow asking you to turn the paper over.

3. Compare your paper to the illustrations for:

- The step you are working on
- The previous step
- The next step, which is your goal

4. Read the directions out loud.

Drawings

For the sake of clarity, the illustrations may increase in size from the beginning of the project to the end. But the angles are always consistent, and you can test your own paper against them.

Measurements

Measurements are given in inches and centimeters, but the conversion may not always be exact in order to avoid awkward fractions. In some cases specific sizes are recommended, but in most cases you may use smaller or larger pieces of paper.

ABOUT PAPER

Most fairly thin, uncoated papers with a crisp surface are suitable for origami. Check out "origami" on the Internet for suppliers of specialty papers. Once you know how to fold an origami, you may want to reproduce it with a paper in a more appropriate color or design, which can make a big difference to the end result.

The following is an overview of the papers most popular with experienced paperfolders.

Origami Paper

Ready-cut squares in varying sizes and colors are available in some art, museum, and gift stores and from catalogs. They are usually colored on one side and white on the other. I recommend 6" (15 cm) as the most versatile all-purpose size. From there you can go on to smaller and larger squares as appropriate for a particular design.

Computer and Bond Paper; Printing Paper in Bright Colors

These types of paper are available in a large assortment of colors at copy shops, office supply stores, and school suppliers. They are sold in size 8 ½" by 11" in packages of 500 sheets (a ream), and are available in two weights, described on the packages as 24 lbs and 20 lbs. The lighter weight paper folds more easily. Printing papers are the most economical choice for schools, youth groups, and other large groups.

Gift Wrap Paper

It is quite difficult to cut paper on rolls into squares, but well worthwhile for special results. Foil gift wrap turns any origami instantly into a festive ornament.

Handmade Paper

This type of paper is softer, but gives rich-looking results. Japanese washi paper in glorious patterns is available in sheets or packages of squares.

Paper Colored on Both Sides

Some projects look better when made from paper that is colored on both sides, such as printing paper. Duo-colored origami squares, sold in packets, have different colors on the front and the back. You can make your own fancy duo papers by gluing sheets of gift wrap or other papers back to back with spray glue or glue sticks.zaper

Recycled Paper

Out-of-date flyers, colorful magazine pages, and other discarded papers can be cut into squares and folded into origami models.

◤ FAQ (Frequently Asked Questions)

What is the history of paperfolding?

"Origami" is a Japanese word consisting of *ori*, meaning to fold, and *gami*, meaning paper. The word has slipped into the English language because paperfolding has spread from Japan, where it is part of the culture. It is known that since the twelfth century paper has been folded in Japan for ceremonial purposes and that in the sixteenth century paper was folded for decorative use and entertainment.

Records show that paper was folded in Europe in the fourteenth century. In the sixteenth and seventeenth centuries it was common practice to fold square baptismal certificates in set patterns.

The kind of recreational origami now popular in Asia and Western countries began in the late nineteenth century, but received its greatest impetus in the latter half of the twentieth century. Akira Yoshizawa in Japan, Lillian Oppenheimer in the United States, and Robert Harbin in England were prominent forces in bringing origami to the attention of the general public.

Is origami art or craft?

Origami is definitely a craft, with an underlying technique, but some models are well recognized as works of art. They have been displayed in major art museums and sold in art galleries.

The most prolific creators seem to have a mathematical, a scientific, or an artistic inclination of which they may not even be aware. Robert Lang and Akira Yoshizawa are two of the foremost artists.

Dr. Robert Lang, an American scientist, designed a now famous cuckoo clock, which requires about 260 intricate folds. He is intrigued by the challenge of devising insects that duplicate their natural details. He has devised the Treemaker software, which bases folding patterns on proportions of the location and size of points on the surface of the paper.

Akira Yoshizawa of Japan is considered the master of artistic origami, which are much admired. His animals seem to come alive and be poised ready to run or jump.

Why fold paper?

Many people find pleasure in the folding process itself when following the diagrams, while others can't wait to achieve the result. Still others enjoy the challenge of inventing entirely new designs and some paperfolders like to teach origami to friends, or in schools and libraries.

Is origami creative?

Paperfolders constantly create new models. Once you know some of the basics, you may begin to create your own simple toys, home decorations, or complex sculptures. They may be variations on existing models or entirely new. Some may appear in just minutes, like a doodle, while others may be so complex that they take months to design and hours to reproduce.

What are some practical uses for origami?

- Entertaining friends and strangers
- Making ornaments and decorations
- Aiding curriculum requirements in math, art, and social science classes
- Fund-raising

How long does it take to learn origami?

You can learn to make a simple model in just a few minutes, while a complex one may be a challenge for many hours. The models in this book vary from simple to intermediate. The more you fold paper, the easier it becomes, in a remarkably short period of time.

At what age can children learn origami?

I have taught three-year-olds on a one-on-one basis, but generally the necessary coordination begins to develop at seven years of age.

How can I teach others?

It's one thing to teach one-on-one in an informal setting and quite another to give a program to a class or other group. In my general introductory programs, I teach groups to make a gift box, a swan, and a leaping frog. I may vary this, depending on special requests by the organizers or the seasons of the year. Before any presentation:

- Decide clearly what you would like to teach.
- Make sure you know how to fold the models, making them over and over until you are familiar with them, verbalizing each step to yourself.
- Prepare the quantity and types of papers you will need, including larger squares for demonstrating up front.

What is the best way to make sharp creases?

Fold the paper on a tabletop or other solid surface. This provides resistance and helps you make straight creases. You can sharpen the creases with your fingernail or an ice-cream stick.

What are the best sizes for models?

Paperfolders call a completed origami a model. Origami models can be made in any size, depending on your own preference. When you make a model for the first time it is best to use a square between 6" to 10" (15 cm to 25 cm). Then you may decide to make the model smaller or larger by using a smaller or larger square to suit the purpose.

What are bases?

Many models begin with the same series of steps, which are called bases. They are recognized by paperfolders all over the world. In **Origami Toys** bases occur in the following models:

- *Kite base:* Jumping Mouse, Monster Mask
- *Blintz base:* Fortune Teller, The Transformer
- *Triangle base:* Wind Toy, Rocket
- *Square base:* A Doll Family, Magic Wand
- *Diamond base:* We Fish, Raven, Two Lovebirds in a Love Boat
- *Fish base:* Dinosaur
- *Housefold base:* Dollhouse, Dollhouse Furniture

What is origami language?

When paperfolders show each other new models they may say: "Begin with the Kite base." The other person will know what to do. These and other terms like valley fold, mountain fold, and so on are shortcuts that keep recurring in origami instructions. In **Origami Toys** I have referred to them as "origami language."

If we accept one dictionary definition of the word "language" as "any mode of communication," then origami itself is a language. When paperfolders find themselves in situations where they have no common language with other people, they often fold and give away an origami bird or toy. They are communicating very well, eliciting smiles and friendship.

Where do models originate?

There are three sources:

- *Traditional*: In many cultures toys are folded from paper, like the dart airplane or the hat made from a newspaper.
- *Known creators*: When paperfolders show or teach models by known creators, they always credit them by name.
- *Unknown creators*: When a model is handed around informally at parties, in schools, and elsewhere, the name of the creator may become lost in the shuffle.

What about copyrights?

You may fold any origami and photocopy printed instructions for your own personal use. You cannot include them in handouts or any printed or electronic format without permission from the creator or copyright holder, which may be a publisher. For more detailed information consult the guidelines provided by OrigamiUSA (see the address at the end of this chapter).

How can I meet other paperfolders?

It's great fun to meet with other paperfolders. Origami clubs where members of all ages meet monthly to exchange directions for models and share other information exist in many localities. OrigamiUSA holds an annual convention in New York City attended by more than 600 enthusiasts from many countries. Other conventions take place in different places. Origami is well represented on the Internet, which can satisfy your curiosity about any of its aspects. Traditional and new designs, whether simple or complex, appear constantly on web sites.

Further Information

Readers interested in learning more about paperfolding can use the keyword "origami" on the Internet. These American and British groups can connect you with other paperfolders in your area or your country:

OrigamiUSA
15 West 77th Street
New York, NY 10024
USA

British Origami Society
2A The Chestnuts
Countesthorpe, Leicester
LE8 5TL, United Kingdom

JUMPING MOUSE

The Jumping Mouse demonstrates origami at its simplest: with just three creases you can convert a paper square into an action toy.

You need:

A 2 ½″ (6 cm) paper square

If the paper is colored on only one side, begin with the white side facing up.

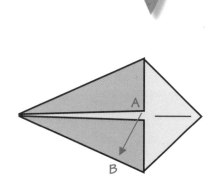

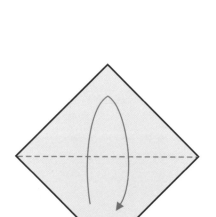

1a. Fold the square from corner to corner.

1b. Unfold it.

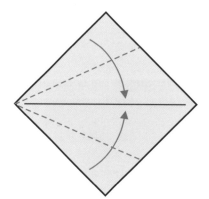

2. Fold two adjacent edges to the crease you just made.

3. In origami language this shape is called a Kite base. Pull corner A to edge B to form a three-dimensional cone.

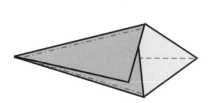

4. Resharpen all creases firmly.

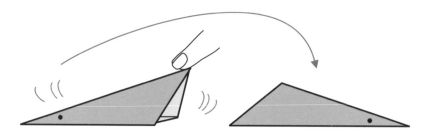

5. Completed Jumping Mouse. Place it on a tabletop. Tap the back corner with your forefinger. Watch it jump!

Better Action

The mouse will somersault even better if the two layers at the bottom are held together with a dab of glue. In any case, the creases must be very sharp.

THE TRANSFORMER

With the Transformer you can amaze your friends by manipulating a large paper square into a pinwheel, a boat, a wallet, a cap, a box, and a lot of other things, with just the flick of the wrist. You fold a Fortune Teller and keep rearranging the existing creases. It's as simple as that.

When I teach origami to groups, I often entertain them by performing the Transformer sequence to show the versatility of a single piece of paper, which most people find fascinating.

You need:

A 16″ (40 cm) paper square, colored on both sides
For practice you can use an 8 ½″ square of colored copying paper.

TRANSFORMER SEQUENCE 1

Preparation Folding

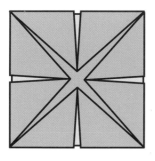

1a. Fold the paper as in Steps 1 through 6 of the Fortune Teller.

1b. Unfold the paper so that it lies flat.

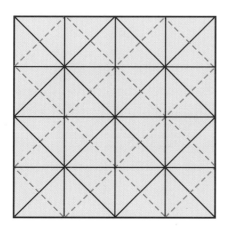

2a. You will have 16 squares on the paper, plus some diagonal creases. Add more diagonal creases so that every one of the 16 squares is crisscrossed with an X.

2b. The square will look as shown here. Fold all horizontal, vertical, and diagonal creases back and forth into valley and mountain folds to make them more flexible. This completes the preparation folding.

Table

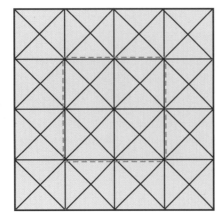

1. Begin with the square unfolded. The four central squares will become the tabletop. Valley fold the creases surrounding the squares sharply.

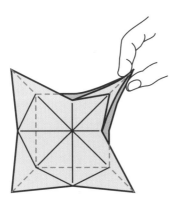

2. Pinch each of the four corners and guide them as far as the tabletop. Then push the sides to meet in the middle. The corners will stick up. Sharpen all creases.

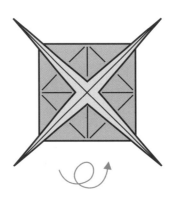

3. Turn the paper over.

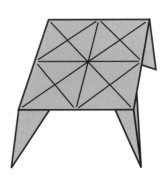

4. Completed Table

Pinwheel

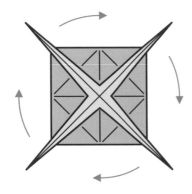

1. With the underside of the Table facing up, arrange all four legs so they rotate to the right.

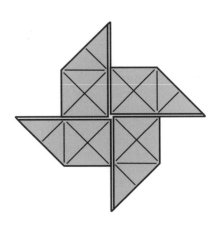

2. Completed Pinwheel

Catamaran Boat

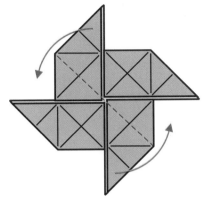

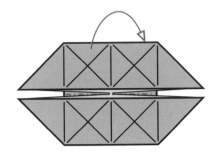

1. On the Pinwheel fold the top flap to the left and the bottom flap to the right.

2. Mountain fold the paper in half to the back.

3. Completed Catamaran Boat

TRANSFORMER SEQUENCE 2 — for Performing Many More Things

Preparation Folding

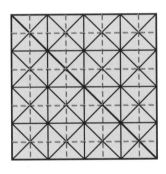

1a. On the same or on another square of paper complete the preparation folding process for Transformer Sequence 1.

1b. Fold horizontal and vertical creases through the middle of all the squares.

1c. Fold all of the creases back and forth (mountain and valley folds).

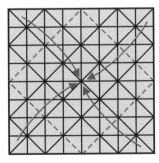

2. On the unfolded square, fold the four corners to the center.

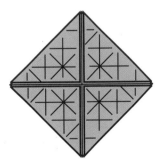

3. Repeat the instructions in Sequence 1 for the Table, the Pinwheel, and the Catamaran Boat, but this time the paper will be double.

Sailboat

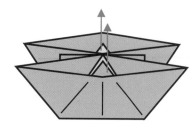

1. Reach inside the Catamaran Boat and pull out the two corners of the original paper square that are hidden inside.

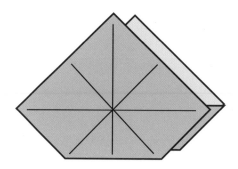

2. Completed Sailboat

Wallet

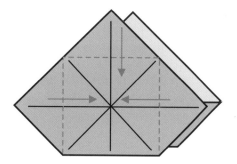

1. Fold the three corners on the front of the Sailboat to the middle. Repeat on the back.

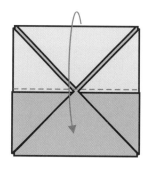

2. Fold all layers at the top down to the front.

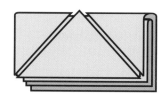

3. Completed Wallet. When you lift the flap that is on the front, you can open the wallet and let your audience see both compartments.

Box

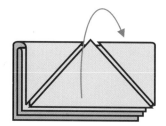

1. Flip the flap on the front of the wallet to the back.

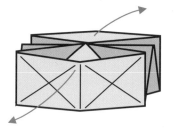

2a. Hold the front and back at the top and pull them gently apart.

2b. Push down the middle to form the box.

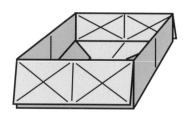

3. Completed Box

Cap

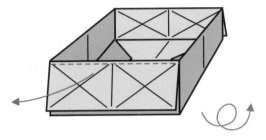 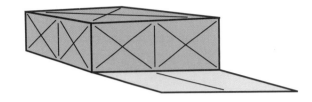

1a. On the Box, swing out one flap for a visor.

1b. Turn the paper upside down.

2. Completed Cap

PRACTICE

As with any performance, practice makes perfect. For a good performance, repeat the folding procedure and spoken patter many times before your presentation. Sequence 1 is intended as an introduction to the more complex Sequence 2. The more you use the Transformer, the better it performs.

PATTER

As with any magic trick the patter that goes along with the performance is very important. It really doesn't matter what you say to introduce each item, as long as you keep talking.

For an ending I usually put on the cap, and say: "And now it's good-bye. I hope you have enjoyed the performance."

MORE TRANSFORMATIONS

Many other objects are hidden in the paper, which you can try to find on your own. Just keep rearranging the creases. So far I have discovered a total of 37, including a star, a bird, a crown, a shirt, and a pair of pants.

PAPER TOYS

In a demonstration all these objects are folded from one piece of paper, but you can also fold them as individual playthings from separate pieces of paper.

◤ MONSTER MASK

With just a few creases, pieces of paper can be changed into origami masks. You may be surprised how easy it is to play fantasy games when disguised as a monster, an animal, a pirate, a rock star, or anyone else.

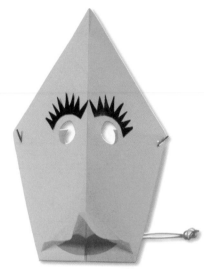

You need:

A 10″ (25 cm) paper square

Scissors

String or elastic

If the paper is colored on only one side, begin with the white side facing up.

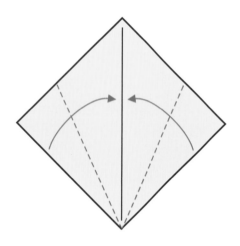

1a. Fold the square from corner to corner. Unfold it.

1b. Fold the outer edges to the crease (kite fold).

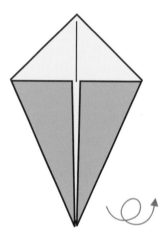

2. Turn the paper over.

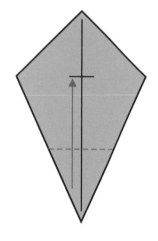

3. Fold the bottom corner up.

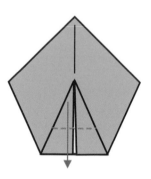

4. Fold the tip down below the bottom edge.

20

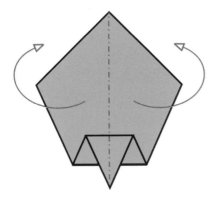

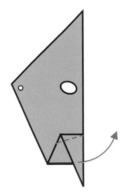

5. Mountain fold the mask in half to the back.

6a. Pull the nose forward, creasing it to make it stick out.

6b. Cut out eyes.

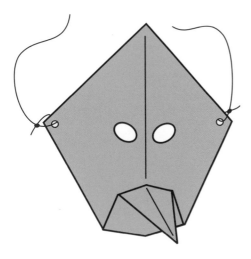

7. Completed Monster Mask. Make a hole on each side of the mask near the eyes. Knot string or elastic on each side and tie at the back of your head.

8. For this mask the top corner has been folded down and cut into hair. The two corners hidden in the back of the mask were folded out for ears, before cutting out the eyes. Try out other changes.

Materials

You can cut up shopping bags to use for making masks. Glue on discarded scraps for additional features.

Fantasy Game and Party

Show guests at a party how to fold the basic mask. Supply paper squares, feathers, stickers, and other add-ons. Ask them to create the desired disguise and interact with each other, pretending to be the personality shown on the mask.

FORTUNE TELLER

The Fortune Teller is one of the best-known playground toys. Because of its simple construction, most people learn how to make it easily.

After you have folded your Fortune Teller, write numbers and predictions onto its four sections. Then, ask others to choose their own preferred numbers and colors, which will predict their fortunes.

Because Fortune Tellers are popular in schools, they are often made from sheets of notebook paper cut into squares, but many other kinds of paper work as well.

You need:

A paper square

If the paper is colored on only one side, begin with the white side facing up.

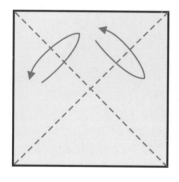

1a. Fold a square from corner to corner, in both directions.

1b. Unfold the paper both times.

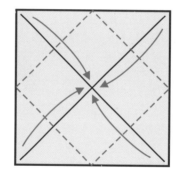

2. Fold the four corners to the center.

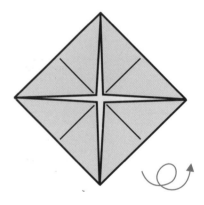

3. In origami language this shape is called a Blintz base. Turn the paper over from front to back.

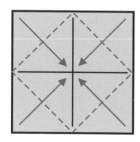

4. Fold the four corners to the center again.

5. Fold the paper in half from side to side. Unfold it.

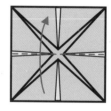

6. Fold the paper in half from bottom to top. Do not unfold it.

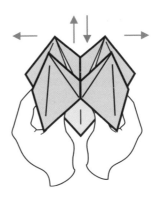

7. Grasp the paper exactly as shown with your thumbs and fingers under the four small squares. Push the four corners together.

8. Completed Fortune Teller. Work it by moving your fingers back and forth, then sideways.

To Tell Fortunes

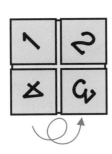

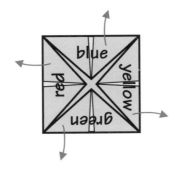

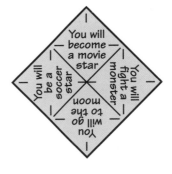

1a. Open the Fortune Teller so that it lies flat, showing four small squares. Write the numbers 1, 2, 3, and 4 on the squares.

1b. Turn the paper over.

2a. It now looks like Step 5 of the instructions. Write four colors on the triangles.

2b. Lift up the triangles.

3a. Write four different predictions in the triangular spaces. Here are some suggestions:

- You will become a movie star
- You will go to the moon
- You will fight monsters
- You will be a soccer star

3b. Refold the Fortune Teller.

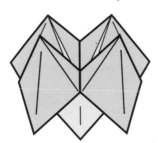

4. Ask someone to select a number from 1 to 4, let's say 3. Open and shut the Fortune Teller three times. Ask the person to choose one of the two colors that show. Lift up that flap and reveal the prediction.

◣ WE FISH!

We Fish! is a good game for a rainy day that anyone of any age can play.

You need:

4″ (10 cm) paper squares

Four 36″ (90 cm) dowel sticks, approximately ¼″ (½ cm) in diameter

String or yarn

Scissors

Christmas ornament hangers or thin wire

A grocery box

A straight pin

If the paper is colored on only one side, begin with the white side facing up.

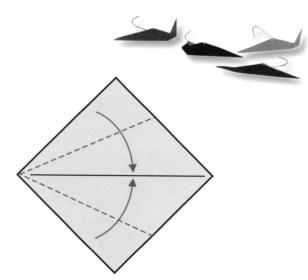

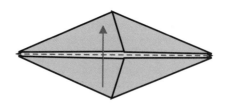

1. For each of the fish, fold a square from corner to corner. Unfold it.

2. Fold two of the adjacent edges to the crease.

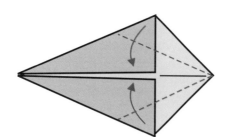

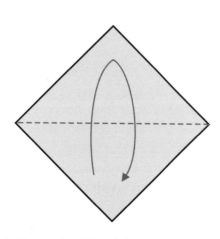

3. Fold the two short edges to the crease.

4. In origami language this shape is called a Diamond base. Fold the paper in half the long way.

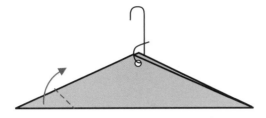

5a. Fold up the tail at an angle.

5b. Pierce a hole at the top of the fish with the straight pin. Attach a Christmas ornament hook or piece of wire bent into a hook shape.

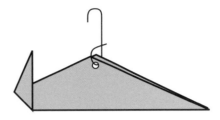

6. Completed Fish

7a. For the fishing rod, cut four pieces of string approximately 20" (45 cm) long. Tie one end of each piece to the end of a dowel. Tie the other end of the string to the closed part of a Christmas ornament hanger. If one is not available, bend a 2 ½" (6 cm) piece of wire into the appropriate shape.

7b. Put a lot of fish into a grocery box left open at the top. Four people at a time can try to hook a fish with their rods. The game is over when all the fish have been lifted out of the box. The person with the most fish is the winner.

More Ideas

You can vary the game depending on the ages of the players. Here are some ideas:

- Players can be blindfolded.
- Fish can be made in different colors, which can carry different points: pink shark equals 5 points, blue fish equals 3 points, gray snapper equals 1 point.
- The folding sequence of the fish can be changed so they look short and squat or longer and pointed.

◣ WIND TOY

This simple toy is easy to make and fun to play with.

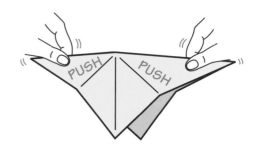

You need:

> *A paper square between 4″ and 6″ (10 cm and 15 cm)*
>
> *A pen or pencil*

If paper is colored on only one side, begin with the colored side facing up.

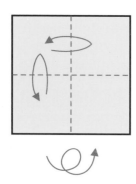

1a. Fold the square in half, both ways. Unfold the paper flat after making each fold.

1b. Turn the paper over.

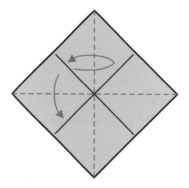

2a. Fold the paper from corner to corner. Unfold it.

2b. Fold the paper corner to corner in the other direction and leave it folded. You will have a triangle.

3. Grasp the paper with both hands at the folded edge in the exact positions shown in the drawing. Move your hands toward each other until the paper forms a triangle. Place it flat on the table.

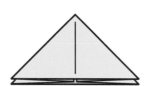

4. In origami language this is called the Triangle or Waterbomb base. Arrange the four flaps in a star shape.

5. Top view. Set the paper on top of a pencil. Blow on it.

6. Completed Wind Toy

◣ DOG PUPPET

Puppets are wonderful toys to stimulate the imagination. Children can make Dog Puppets and talk about their own pets or pets they would like to have.

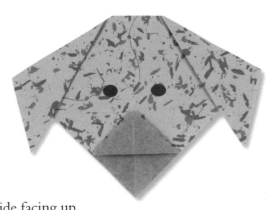

You need:

> ***A paper square***

If the paper is colored on only one side, begin with the white side facing up.

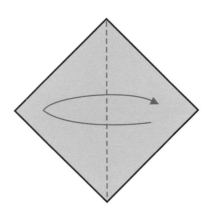

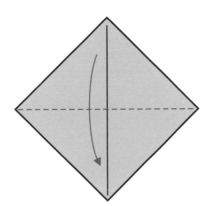

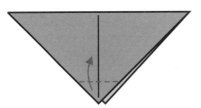

1. Fold the square from corner to corner. Unfold it.

2. Fold the square from corner to corner in the other direction. Do not unfold.

3. Fold one layer of the bottom corner up.

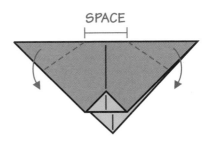

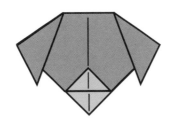

4. Fold two corners down for ears so that they peek over the side edges.

5. Completed Dog Puppet. Hold the puppet at both ears and push your hands together and apart to make the dog "bark."

Paper Party

At a birthday party, show guests how to make the Dog Puppet and invite them to invent other animals by changing the position of the ears.

◣ AIRPLANE

The airplane shown here is a variation on the traditional dart. It's easy to fold and you can have more fun by experimenting in making it glide or fly a long distance, or perhaps even boomerang. It's all about aerodynamics.

You need:

> **A piece of paper 8 ½" x 11" (or A4 size)**
>
> **Sticky tape**

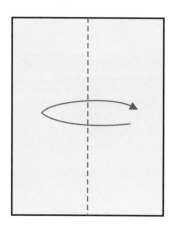

1. Fold the paper in half the long way. Unfold it.

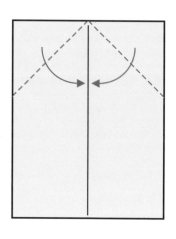

2. Fold the top corners to the crease.

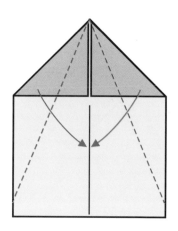

3. Bring the slanted folded edges to the long crease.

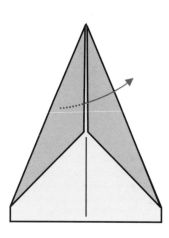

4. Reach inside on the left fold and pull out the hidden corner of the paper.

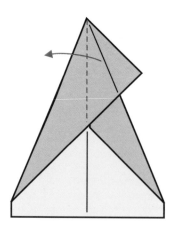

5. Fold the corner over to the other side.

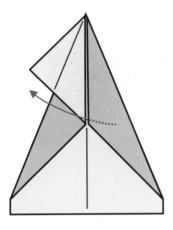

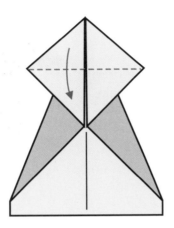

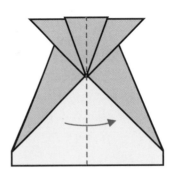

6. Repeat Steps 4 and 5 with the other hidden corner on the right.

7. Fold the top corner down.

8. Fold the plane in half.

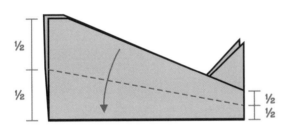

½

½

½
½

9. On the front, fold the long slanted edge to the bottom. See the next drawing. Repeat this on the back.

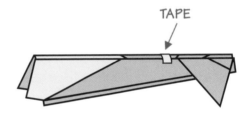

TAPE

10. Loosen the wings so they stick out to the sides. Put a piece of sticky tape where shown.

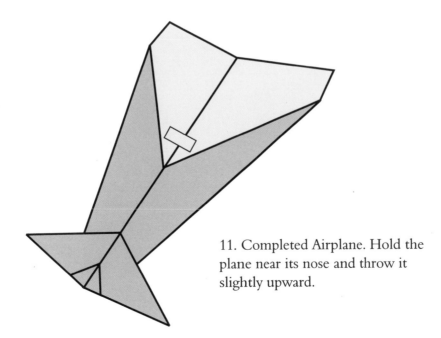

11. Completed Airplane. Hold the plane near its nose and throw it slightly upward.

◥ LEAPING FROG

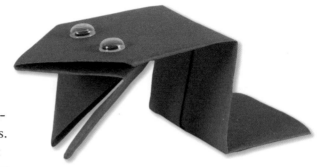

The Leaping Frog is probably the most popular origami toy, appealing to adults and children alike. Adults can fold their business cards into frogs as easy conversation icebreakers, especially during tedious waiting times. Children like to compete, seeing who can flip the most into a bowl. Either way, the frog always produces smiles.

You need:

A 5″ x 3″ index card or a business card

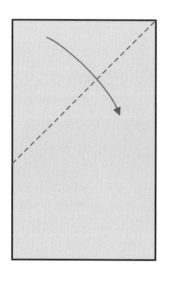

1. Fold the short, top edge to the long edge, making the crease through the right, top corner. Unfold it.

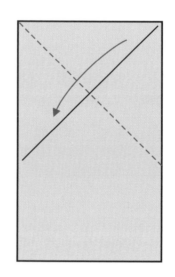

2. Fold the short, top edge to the opposite long edge, making the crease through the left, top corner. Unfold it.

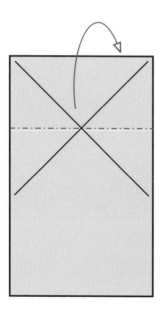

3. You will see an X on the paper. Mountain fold to the back right through the middle of the X.

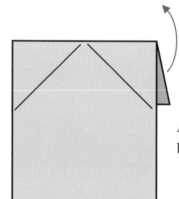

4. Flip up the back layer.

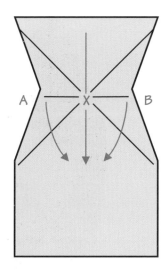

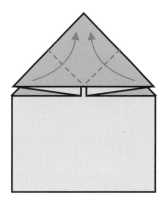

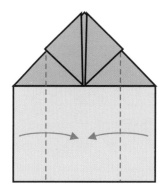

5. Push down on the middle of the X. Then, grasp both sides of the paper and bring A and B together in the middle. Flatten the top of the paper into a triangle. See the next drawing.

6. Fold the outer corners of the triangle to the top corner.

7. Fold the sides to the middle.

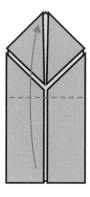

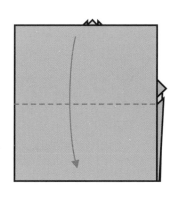

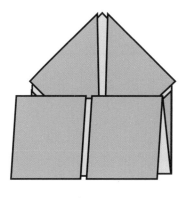

8. Fold the bottom edge up to the top corner.

9. Bring the same edge down again to the bottom.

10. Completed Leaping Frog

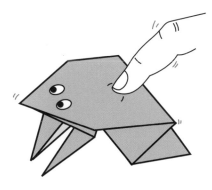

11. Set the frog into a good jumping position by loosening the front and back legs. Tap the frog's back and it will jump. Some frogs like to somersault.

◤ ROCKET

Blast off for a space-age party with this rocket. It looks best when made from shiny silver gift wrap.

You need:

A paper square

If the paper is colored on only one side, begin with colored sid facing up.

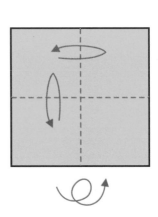

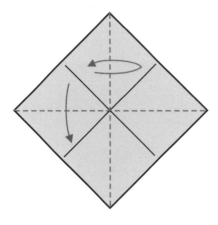

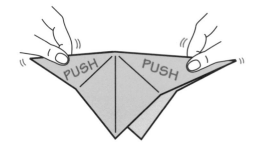

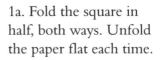

1a. Fold the square in half, both ways. Unfold the paper flat each time.

1b. Turn the paper over.

2a. Fold and unfold the square from corner to corner.

2b. Fold the square from corner to corner in the other direction and leave it folded. You will have a triangle.

3. Grasp the paper with both hands at the folded edge in the exact positions shown. Move your hands toward each other until the paper forms a triangle. Place it flat on the table.

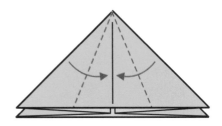

4a. Make sure the triangle has two flaps on each side. If you have only one flap on one side and three on the other, flip one flap over.

4b. In origami language this shape is called a Triangle or Waterbomb base. Fold the outer edges of both front flaps to the middle. Turn the paper over and repeat on the back.

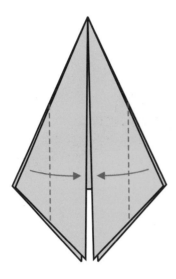

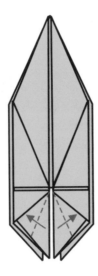

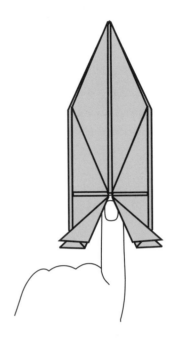

5a. Fold the outer corners to the middle.

5b. Turn the paper over and repeat this on the back.

6. Fold the bottom points out. Repeat this on the back.

7. Poke your finger into the rocket and open it gently.

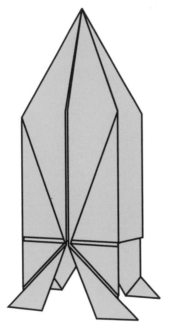

8. Completed Rocket

Ready for Countdown

Rockets make unusual party favors or place cards, when you glue on small labels with guests' names written on them. To make invitations, fold rockets but leave them flat by omitting Step 7. Glue them on note cards.

Space Travel Game

Suspend a hula hoop from the ceiling. If a hula hoop is not available, you can pull a wire hanger into a circle. Let everyone fold a rocket. Throw the rockets to the moon (hula hoop). Make rules about how to win points.

◣ DINOSAUR

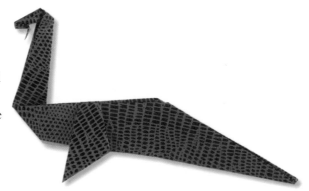

You can populate prehistoric landscapes with big origami dinosaurs folded from large paper squares. For mini-dinosaurs use small paper squares. Follow the same folding pattern and glue the dinosaurs on pieces of construction paper or blank cards for party invitations.

You need:

A paper square

If the paper is colored on only one side, begin with the white side facing up.

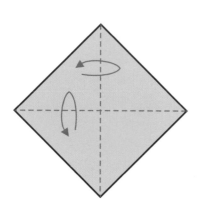

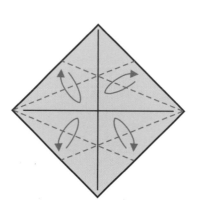

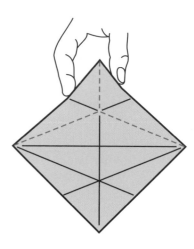

1. Fold a square from corner to corner in both directions. Unfold it each time.

2. Fold all four edges to the diagonal crease, in turn, unfolding them each time.

3a. Pinch the top corner between your thumb and forefinger and guide the paper so that it lies on the two creases made in Step 2. See the next drawing .

3b. Repeat this process with the bottom corner.

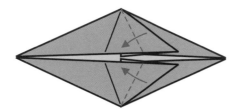

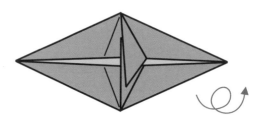

4. Fold the two short slanted edges to the middle, as shown. They will overlap.

5. Turn the paper over.

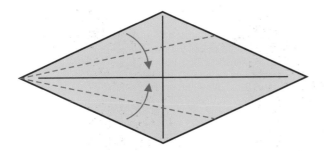

6. Fold the two slanted edges to the long middle crease.

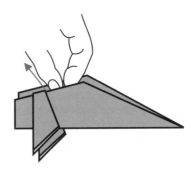

7. Form the neck with a valley fold.

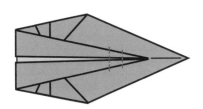

8. Form the head with two more valley folds.

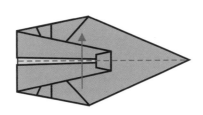

9. Valley fold the paper in half the long way. The legs will swing out.

10. Let the paper open slightly. Reach inside and lift up the neck until it is almost vertical. To make it stay in place, crease the short edge at the front sharply.

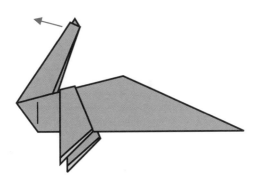

11. Pull the head forward. Crease the paper sharply at the back of the head to make it stay in place.

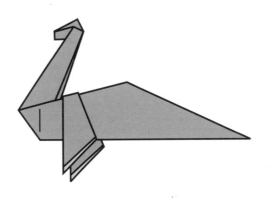

12. Completed Dinosaur

◣ RAVEN

The Raven is an entertaining action toy that opens and shuts its beak. Parents and librarians like to use it for telling stories, but children can have fun letting it invent a fantastic tale.

You need:

A paper square

If the paper is colored on only one side, begin with the white side facing up.

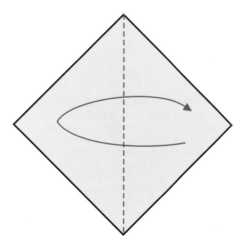

1. Fold a square from corner to corner. Unfold it.

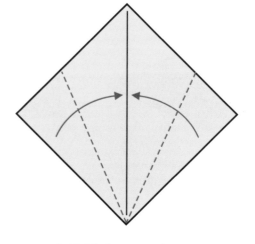

2. Fold the two adjacent edges to the crease.

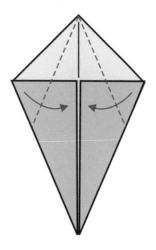

3. Fold the two short edges to the crease.

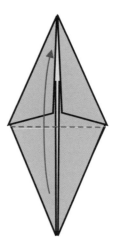

4. In origami language this shape is called a Diamond base. Fold the paper in half.

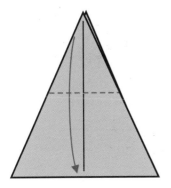

5. Fold the top corner of the front flap only to the bottom edge.

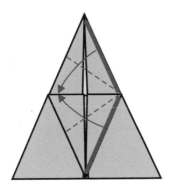

6. Fold the two edges marked with thick red lines to the middle crease.

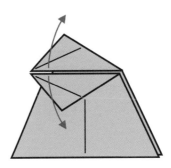

7. Unfold the two creases made in Step 6.

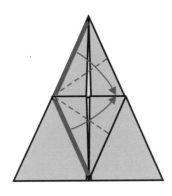

8. Fold the two edges marked with thick red lines to the middle crease.

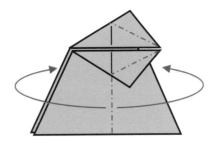

9. Mountain fold the bottom half of the paper in half, to the back. Let the Raven's beak settle into the creases made in Steps 6 and 8.

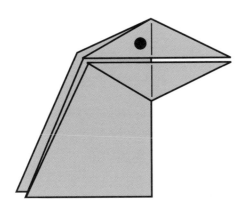

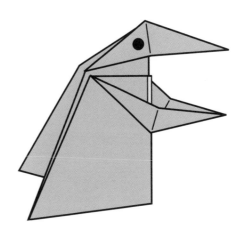

10. Completed Raven. To make it open its beak and caw, pull the sides apart. You can add your own sound effects.

TWO LOVE BIRDS IN A LOVE BOAT

The Two Love Birds will kiss each other when you pull the sides of the boat apart.

You need:

An 8″ (20 cm) paper square

If the paper is colored on only one side, begin with the white side facing up.

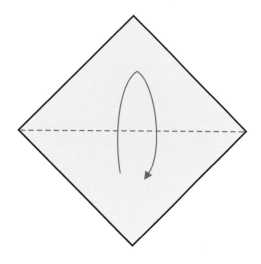

1. Fold a square from corner to corner. Unfold it.

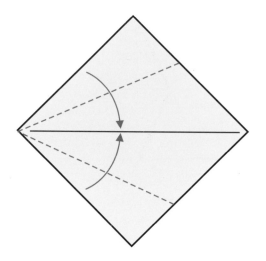

2. Fold the two adjacent edges to the crease.

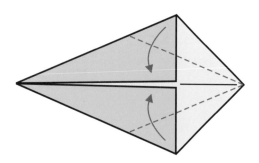

3. Fold the two short edges to the crease.

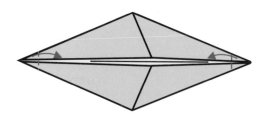

4. In origami language this shape is called a Diamond base. Fold in the two outside corners.

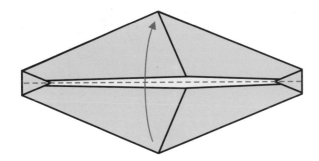

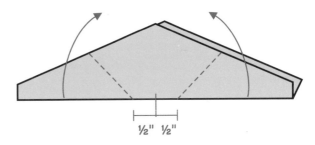

5. Fold the paper in half the long way.

6. Fold the outside corners straight up. Note that each crease begins ½" (1 cm) away from the middle.

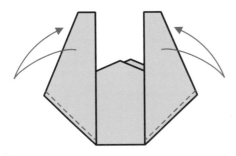

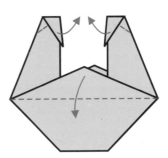

7. Unfold Step 6 and reverse fold on the same creases, bringing the paper in between the two main layers. In origami language this is called an inside reverse fold.

8a. Pull the heads toward each other, making creases at the back of the heads. You have made and outside reverse fold.

8b. Fold the middle corners down, first on the front, then repeat this on the back. These will be the handles.

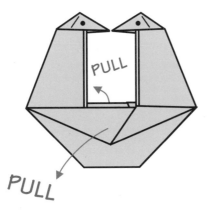

9. Completed Two Love Birds in a Love Boat. When you pull the handles on either side of the boat apart and together, the birds will kiss each other.

Table Decoration

The Love Birds can be used as table decorations. Form a stand by making a crease ¼" (½ cm) away from the bottom edge, then let the boat open up a little, exposing a rectangle. Mountain fold all four lines of the rectangle and push it up. Flatten the rectangle so that the boat can stand on its own or you can glue it on a small piece of cardboard, which can also serve as a place card.

▲ HYDROFOIL

When you blow on this origami model, it skims over a smooth tabletop like a hydrofoil that skims over the surface of the water. Hydrofoil boats travel above the water on an air cushion. They may be single-passenger fun boats for exciting competitive water sports or larger ships used by the military or to carry passengers.

You need:

A piece of paper 8 ½″ x 11″ (or A4 size)

Scissors

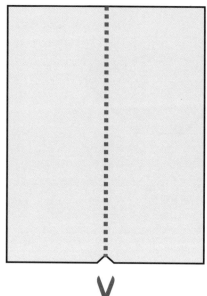

1. Cut the paper in half the long way. Each piece will make a hydrofoil.

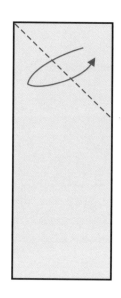

2. Fold the short, top edge to the opposite long edge, making the crease through the left, top corner. Unfold it.

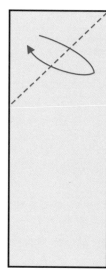

3. Fold the short, top edges to the opposite long edge, making the crease through the right, top corner. Unfold it.

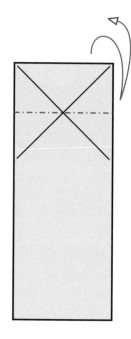

4. The creases form an X on the paper. Mountain fold the paper to the back through the middle of the X. Unfold it.

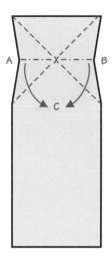  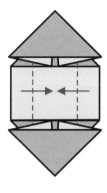

5. Push down on the middle of the X. Then, grasp both sides of the paper at the ends of the crease. Bring A and B together in the middle at C. Flatten the top of the paper into a triangle. See the next drawing.

6. Repeat Steps 2–5 on the other end of the paper.

7. Fold the straight outside edges to the middle, tucking them under the triangles.

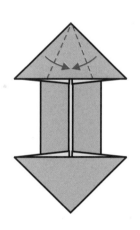 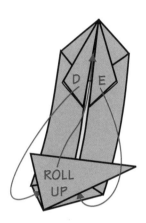

8. Fold the slanted edges of the triangle at the top to the middle.

9a. Roll the bottom corner up. Then slide points D and E in between the two layers of paper.

9b. When D and E are pushed in as far as possible flatten the paper and make a new crease at the bottom edge. See next drawing.

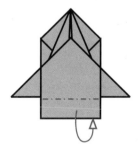 

10. Mountain fold the paper across the bottom and let the newly formed rectangle extend down at a right angle.

11. Completed Hydrofoil. Blow on the back to propel it across the tabletop.

Competition

Show your friends how to fold hydrofoils and have races with them.

FOOTBALL GAME

Play a game of football anytime, anywhere with any handy piece of paper.

You need:

A piece of paper 8 ½″ x 11″ (or A4)

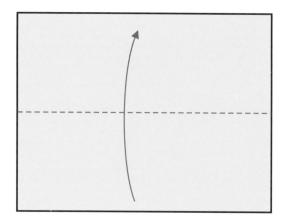

1. Fold the paper in half the long way.

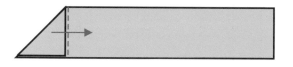

2. Fold it in half again.

3. Valley fold the corner, lining up the short edge on the long edge.

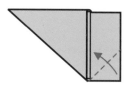

4. Fold the triangle over.

5. Keep folding over triangles, almost to the end of the strip.

6. Fold the corner up.

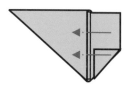

7. Tuck the leftover piece in between the layers of the bulky triangle.

8. Completed Football

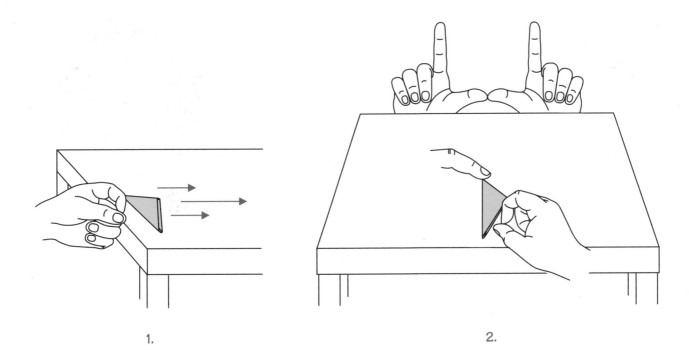

1.   2.

Rules of the Game for Two Players

1. A tabletop is the field. Mark off areas at both ends of the table where a player will make a touchdown if the football lands there.

2. Place the football flat at one end of the table. The first player flicks the football with his or her forefinger toward the opposite edge.

- If the football lands in the marked touchdown area, the player scores one point.
- If the football remains on the table, but does not land in the marked area, the other player takes a turn at flicking it in the opposite direction.
- If the football falls off the edge, the opponent starts it near the edge where it fell off.

3. After scoring a point the player is entitled to try for a conversion. The opponent forms goalposts by placing both wrists on the table, thumbs next to each other and forefingers up. This time, place the football on one of its points and "kick" it by flicking it up in the air over the thumbs and between the fingers. If successful, the player scores a field goal worth two points.

Of course, players can invent other rules, including time limits.

◣ BASKETBALL GAME

You can practice basketball skills with a hoop and ball made from paper.

You need:

   A piece of paper 8 ½″ x 11″ (or A4 size)

   Tissue paper squares with 4″ (10 cm) sides, one for each player

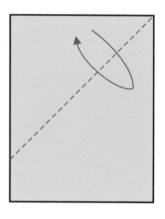

1. Fold the short, top edge to the long edge, making the crease through the top right corner. Unfold it.

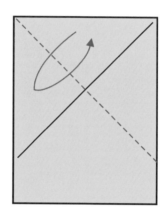

2. Fold the short, top edge to the opposite long edge making the crease through the top left corner. Unfold it.

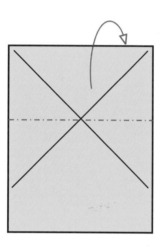

3. You will see an X on the paper. Mountain fold to the back, through the middle of the X.

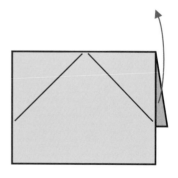

4. Flip up the back layer.

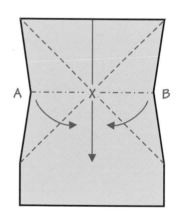

5. Push down on the middle of the X. Then grasp both sides of the paper and bring A and B together in the middle. Flatten the top of the paper into a triangle. See the next drawing.

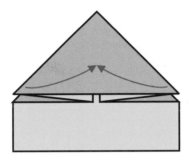 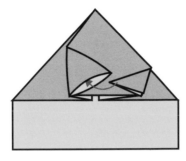 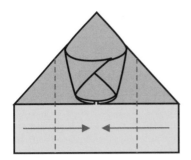

6. Form the basket by bringing the outside corners to the middle.

7. Push the right corner in between the two layers of the left corner. See the next drawing.

8. Fold both sides to the middle. Then release them at right angles to form a stand.

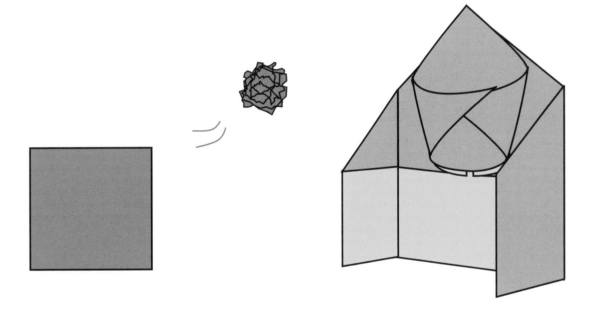

9. Crumple up the tissue paper squares tightly.

10. Completed Basketball Hoop

How to Play

Decide on the distance from which to throw the "ball." Score a point each time it goes into the basket. If it always goes in, then increase the distance. If you are playing against a friend, make up your own rules.

Party Decorations

Set a basketball hoop at each place setting and spread candies around.

◣ MAGIC ROTATOR

A strip of paper can be twisted in such a way that three different designs appear at each turn. You have the choice of decorating the three faces with colors, numbers, pictures, or even a message. You need fairly strong paper that will last through many rotations, or you can use adding machine tape. For this toy to work well, it is important to fold it accurately.

Mathematicians have been fascinated with this kind of movable ring, which is called a flexagon.

You need:

> *A strip of paper or a piece of adding machine tape 15″ x 2 ¼″ (38 cm x 6 cm)*
>
> *Scissors*
>
> *Glue*
>
> *Markers in red, green, and yellow*

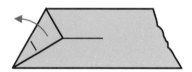

1. At one end of the strip, find the middle of the short edge by bringing the long edges together and making a long pinch mark.

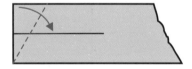 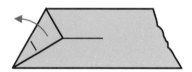 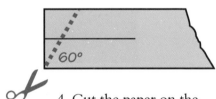

2. Fold the upper-left corner so that it lies on the pinch mark. Note that the crease begins at the bottom corner.

3. Unfold Step 2.

4. Cut the paper on the slanted crease. You have a 60-degree angle.

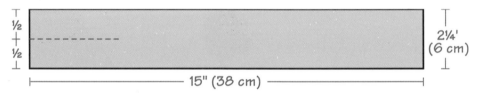

5a. Fold the slanted edge to the top edge. The crease goes right through the top corner.

5b. Using the triangle as a guide, keep folding the strip back and forth like an accordion, until you have ten triangles.

6a. Cut off any excess paper.

6b. Open the paper so that it lies flat.

46

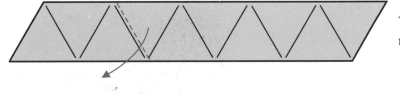

7. Valley fold the paper on the crease next to the third triangle, as shown.

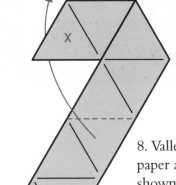

8. Valley fold the paper again, as shown, and fold the strip behind triangle X.

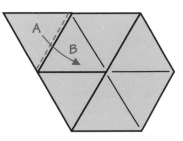

9. Fold triangle A on to triangle B, and glue them together.

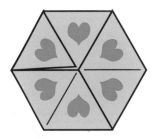

10a. Put a heart on each of the triangles on the front.

10b. Turn the rotator over, and draw flowers on the triangles on the back.

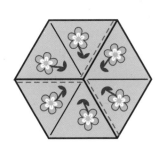

11. Now rotate the ring like this: You will see cut edges on the left sides of three triangles. Bring these three edges together, letting the three pinched corners meet in the middle.

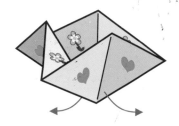

12a. Magically, you can now separate the bottom of the paper and let it lie flat again.

12b. The rotator face will be blank. Color it with six stars.

13. Completed Magic Rotator. To expose the three different faces in turn, keep repeating Steps 11 and 12, always bringing the cut edges together.

Amazing Math

By following Steps 1 to 3 on the edge of any piece of paper you can create a 60-degree angle!

Geometric Designs

Experiment by decorating the three surfaces with different lines, angles, or curves.

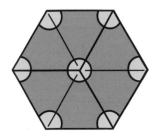

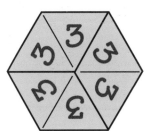

◣ TIC TAC TOE GAME

Many games can be played on this origami Tic Tac Toe Board, which can be carried around in a plastic bag.

You need:

> *A paper square 9″ (21 cm) or larger, for the board*
>
> *5 purple 1 ½″ (4 cm) paper squares, for markers*
>
> *5 yellow 1 ½″ (4 cm) paper squares, for markers*
>
> *A ruler*

FOR THE BOARD

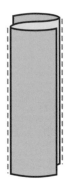

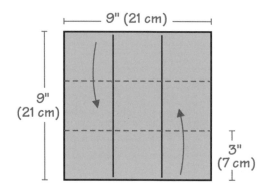

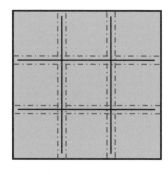

1. Fold the large square into thirds. Find the crease lines by rolling the paper as shown, and wiggle it until all three layers are equal. Then crease it.

2a. Unfold the paper and crease it into thirds again, this time across the paper.

2b. Unfold the paper flat. The square now has four creases, two in each direction.

3. If the paper is colored on only one side, let the colored side face up. Make mountain folds ¼″ (½ cm) away on both sides of all four creases. Unfold them each time.

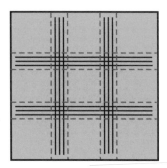

4a. Make two valley folds ¼″ (½ cm) away from all the mountain folds. Unfold them each time.

4b. Arrange each band of five creases into a box pleat. See the profile view. First do both vertical bands using the existing mountain and valley folds. Fold the horizontal bands right across them.

PROFILE VIEW

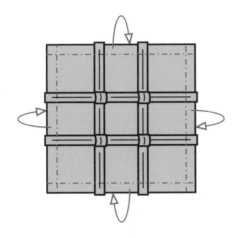

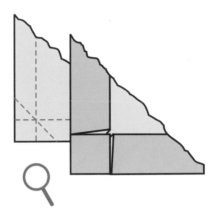

5. Mountain fold all outside edges about ½" (1 cm) to the back.

6. Optional: For a neater finish squash fold the four corners on the underside of the board.

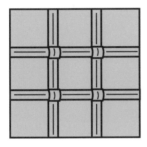

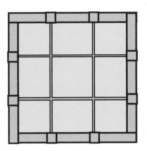

7. Completed Tic Tac Toe Board

8. Underside

FOR MARKERS

Fold all ten squares in the same way.

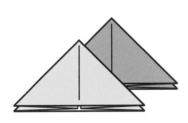

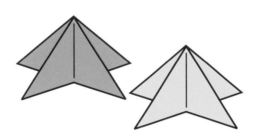

1a. Fold Steps 1 through 3 of the Rocket. You will have a triangle with two flaps on each side.

1b. Arrange the triangle into a three-dimensional star shape.

2. Completed Marker

3. Top view

 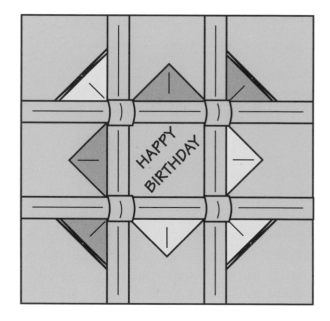

How to Play the Tic Tac Toe Game

Two players alternate in placing markers on the board. Whoever is able to place three markers in a row, either across the board, up and down, or on the diagonals, is the winner.

Storage, Mailing, and Greeting Cards

Tuck the markers into the ridges of the Tic Tac Toe Board. This makes it easy to store and easy to mail. You can also write a greeting in the central square: "Happy Birthday" or whatever else suits the occasion.

Quilt Block Patterns

You can tuck the markers into the ridges in many different patterns. Here are examples of two possible patterns.

◣ DOLLHOUSE

It is easy to create an origami dollhouse and equip it with origami furniture. It can provide hours of fun in the making and during subsequent playtime. Any kind of strong paper is suitable. Recycled shopping bags provide excellent material.

Dollhouses fascinate not only children, but also adults. Many collectors and hobbyists own miniature homes, which they equip with authentically reproduced furnishings.

You need:

A 15″ (40 cm) square of brown wrapping paper • Marker

If the paper is colored on only one side, begin with the white side facing up.

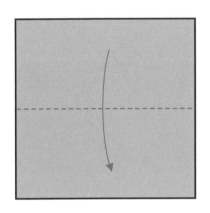

1. Fold a square in half.

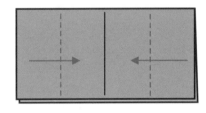

2. Fold it in half again, the short way. Unfold it.

3. Fold the outer edges to the middle crease.

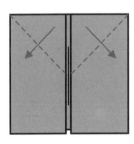

4. Fold the corners from the middle to the outer edges.

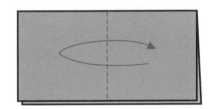

5. Pull the single top layer of the paper outward at X, at the same time squash the top into a roof.

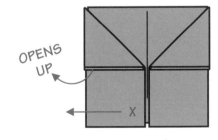

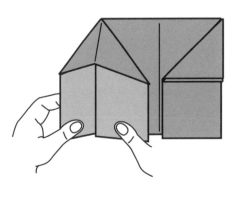

6. This shows Step 5 in progress.

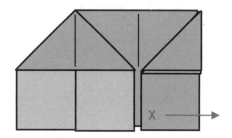

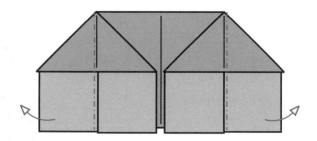

7. Repeat Step 5 on the right-hand side.

8. Arrange both ends so they are at right angles to the middle part. In origami language this shape is called the Housefold base.

9. Completed Dollhouse. Draw a door and windows.

◤ DOLLHOUSE FURNITURE

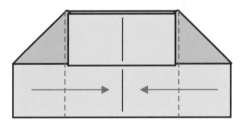

You can fill the origami dollhouse with paper furniture for many hours of play. The instructions show how to fold a sofa, a piano, and a dresser.

Furniture reproductions have been found in early Egyptian tombs, but during the nineteenth century owning and displaying completely furnished dollhouses became a very popular hobby. They are often reproduced on a scale of one inch to one foot of actual size.

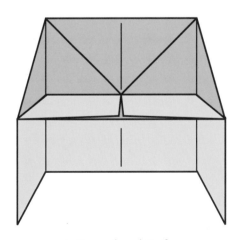

To furnish the origami dollhouse made from a 15" (40 cm) paper square, use 3" (7 cm) squares for the furniture, but it is better to practice first with larger squares.

You need:

3 paper squares

If the paper is colored on only one side, begin with the white side facing up.

FOR THE SOFA

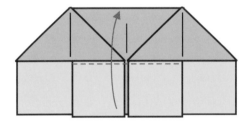

1a. Fold a square following Steps 1 through 7 of the Dollhouse.

1b. Fold the middle part up to the top edge.

2. Fold the sides in.

3. Pull the middle flap down so that it sticks straight out to the front. The sides will also move forward.

4. Completed Sofa

FOR THE PIANO

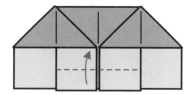

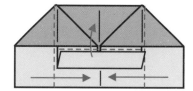

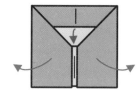

1a. Fold a square following Steps 1 through 7 of the Dollhouse.

1b. Fold the middle part up so that it lies against the bottom of the roof.

2a. Fold the middle part up again.

2b. Fold the sides in.

3. Open both sides and the middle part so that they stick straight out to the front.

4. Completed Piano

Optional: You can draw on keys and narrow the sides by folding them in half.

FOR THE DRESSER

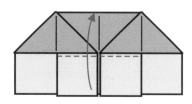

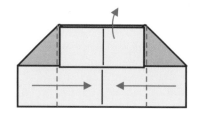

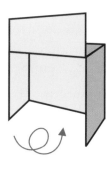

1a. Fold a square following Steps 1 through 7 of the Dollhouse.

1b. Fold the middle part up to the top edge.

2. Pull the middle flap up so that it extends above the house roof. As you pull, the sides will move so that they stick out toward you. See the next drawing.

3. Turn the paper over. Sharpen all of the creases.

4. Completed Dresser

Other furnishings

Try to invent other pieces of origami furniture, such as a table, a chair, or a television set.

Paper Town

For a group project create a town with many furnished dollhouses.

◣ A DOLL FAMILY

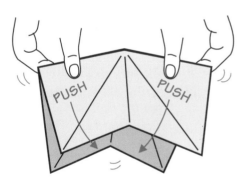

In most cultures dolls are basic toys that seem to satisfy a deep human need. They come in all sizes, representing children or adults of both sexes. They may be as simple as a few twigs covered with scraps of fabric or as elaborate as portraits of real people dressed in fashionable clothes that are highly valued by collectors.

You can make an origami paper doll family that can provide fun in the making and many hours of play. The father, mother, and children are all made up of three similar parts that slide into each other. For the upper and lower bodies select colored or small-patterned papers, which give the appearance of clothing. For the heads select plain pink paper. For doll children use smaller paper squares than for adults.

You need, for each doll:

> *Two 8″ (20 cm) paper squares, for the body*
>
> *One 4″ (10 cm) paper square, for the head*
>
> *One 5″ (12 cm) paper doily for the skirt*

If the paper is colored on only one side, begin with the white side facing up.

FOR THE HEAD

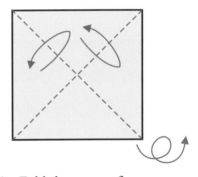

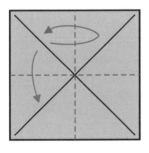

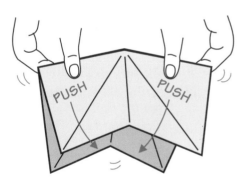

1a. Fold the square from corner to corner in both directions. Unfold the paper so that it lies flat each time.

1b. Turn the paper over.

2a. Fold the paper in half, and unfold it.

2b. Fold the paper in half the other way and leave it folded.

3. Grasp the paper with both hands at the folded edge in the exact positions shown in the drawing. Move your hands toward each other until the paper forms a square. Place it flat on the table.

55

CLOSED CORNER

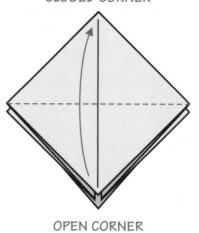

OPEN CORNER

4a. Make sure the square has two flaps on each side. If you have only one flap on one side and three on the other, flip one flap over. In origami language this shape is called the Square or Preliminary base.

4b. Place the paper with the open corner facing toward you.

4c. Fold the single layer of paper up, first on the front, then on the back.

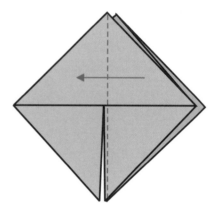

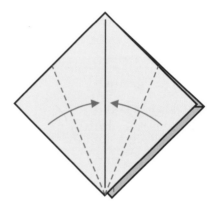

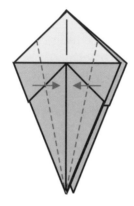

5a. Fold the right front flap over to the left, like the page of a book.

5b. Turn the paper over and repeat the process on the back, again folding from the right to the left.

6. Fold the right and left lower sides to the middle, front flaps only. Repeat this on the back.

7. Fold the long edges to the middle. Repeat this on the back. (Omit this step for a wider head.)

8a. Fold the right side over to the left, as if you are turning the page of a book.

8b. Turn the paper over and repeat the process on the back, again folding from right to left.

9. Completed Head

FOR THE LOWER BODY

1a. Fold one of the larger squares following the steps for the Head.

1b. Fold the feet out with reverse folds.

2. Completed Lower Body

FOR THE UPPER BODY

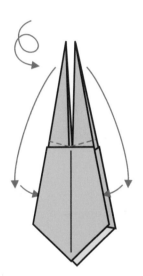

1a. Fold one of the larger squares just like the Head.

1b. Turn the paper upside down.

1c. Valley fold the arms to the sides.

1d. Unfold the valley fold in Step 1c and reverse fold the arms by pushing them in between the main layers of the paper on the creases made previously.

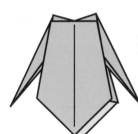

2. Completed Upper Body

Assembly

1a. Slide the Head into the top of the Upper Body.

1b. Slide the Lower Body into the Upper Body.

1c. For a skirt cut the doily in half. Fold it into a pie slice. Tuck it under the Upper Body.

2. Completed Doll Family

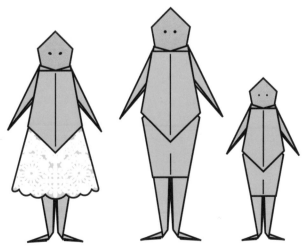

GUM WRAPPER CHAIN

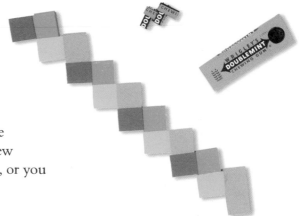

At one time it was a fad for high-school students to make chains from empty gum wrappers and compete to have the longest one. These chains are fun to make. You can add new links by collecting gum wrappers as they become available, or you can construct the same kind of chain with plain paper.

You need:

Gum wrappers or paper rectangles of the same size: 2″ x 2⁵/₈″ (5 cm x 6¹/₂ cm)

Scissors

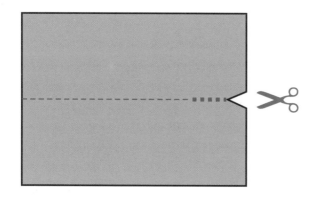

1. Unfold a gum wrapper so that it lies flat. Fold it in half the long way. Cut the paper on the crease. Each half will make one link.

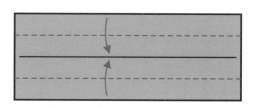

2a. Fold one of the strips in half the long way. Unfold it.

2b. Bring both long edges to the crease.

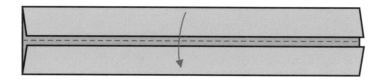

3. Fold the paper in half the long way.

4a. Fold the paper in half the short way. Unfold it.

4b. Fold the short ends to the middle, leaving a small gap in between.

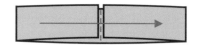

5. Fold the paper in half.

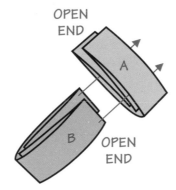
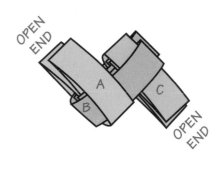

6a. This completes one link.

6b. Fold a few more links.

7. Assemble the chain like this:

Place the arms of link B in between the layers of the arms of link A.

8. Place the arms of link C in the arms of link B, forming a zigzag.

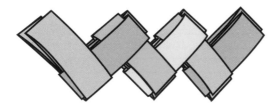

9. Continue adding links in the same way, until the chain is as long as you like.

Jewelry

You can make necklaces and bracelets with gum wrappers. When you alternate papers in two or more different colors, an attractive pattern emerges.

Size

Links made from gum wrappers are quite small. If you make them from larger pieces of paper the chain will grow longer much faster. The strips of paper must be in the same proportion as the gum wrappers. If you use strips of paper, 6" x ¾" (14 cm x 1 ½ cm), begin making each link with Step 4a.

Unit Origami

The gum wrapper chain is a good example of Unit Origami or Modular Origami. In this technique, a number of pieces of paper are all folded alike and combined into boxes, toys, or other objects.

Trivia

The Guinness World Record for the longest gum wrapper chain is held by Canadian Gary Duschl. His chain is made up of 940,510 gum wrappers, is 40,416 ft long, or as long as 37 football fields. And he is still working on it!

The linking technique has also been used for constructing picture frames, purses, and boxes.

◥ MAGIC WAND

Magic Wands make wonderful party favors. Each one is made up of a square of paper folded into a star, supported on a stick made from a long strip of paper.

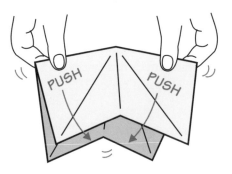

You need:

> **An 8″ (20 cm) paper square**
>
> **A strip of construction paper 2″ x 15″ (5 cm x 35 cm)**

If the paper is colored on only one side, begin with the white side facing up.

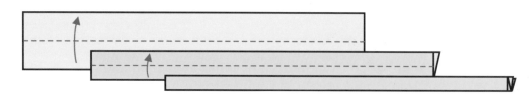

1. Fold the strip in half the long way.

2. Fold it in half again.

3. Completed strip. Put it aside.

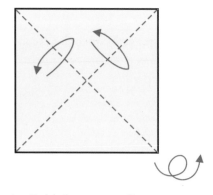

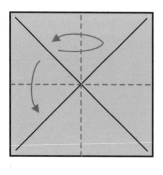

4a. Fold the square from corner to corner in both directions. Unfold the paper so that it lies flat each time.

4b. Turn the paper over.

5a. Fold the paper in half, and unfold it.

5b. Fold it in half the other way, but leave it folded.

6. Grasp the paper with both hands at the folded edge in the exact position shown in the drawing. Move your hands toward each other until the paper forms a square. Place it flat on the table.

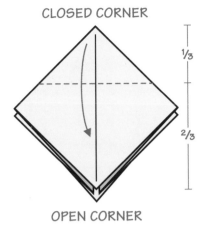

CLOSED CORNER

⅓

⅔

OPEN CORNER

7a. Make sure that the square has two flaps on each side. If you have only one flap on one side and three flaps on the other, flip one flap over. In origami language this shape is called the Square or Preliminary base.

7b. Place the paper with the open corner facing toward you.

7c. Fold the closed corner down about one-third of the way.

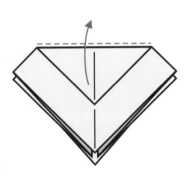

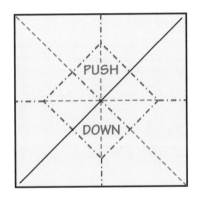

PUSH

DOWN

NOTE:
• Mountain folds are shown as green
• Valley folds are shown as red
• Previous fold lines (which do not get re-folded in this step) are shown as black

8a. Fold the corner up again.

8b. Open the paper.

9a. Crease sharp mountain folds on the small square in the middle.

9b. Press down on the center, and refold the paper into all the creases of the square base. The top corner will be hidden. In origami language this move is called a sink fold.

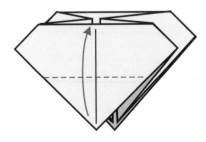

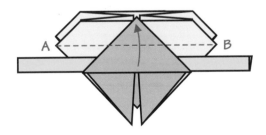

A B

10. Fold the bottom corner of front flap only up to the top edge.

11a. Place the strip inside the triangle.

11b. Bring the folded edge up with the strip inside. The crease goes from corner A to corner B.

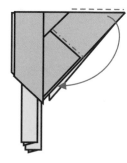

12a. Swing the bottom corners to touch the left and right outside corners A and B. Part of the creases are made under the middle triangle.

12b. Then reverse fold the same two corners like this: Unfold them and then fold them in between the next two layers of paper. They will disappear.

13. Mountain fold the paper in half, to the back.

14. Hide the corner with a reverse fold by lining it up inside with the other layers. The paper will open up while you are doing this.

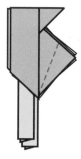

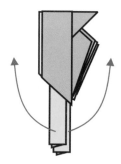

15a. There are six flaps on the right. Fold each flap to the left.

15b. Reverse fold the six flaps like this: Unfold the flaps made in Step 15a, and then fold the flaps in between the next two layers of paper. They will disappear.

16. Completed Magic Wand, shown closed. Swing the ends of the paper strips apart and around so that they touch each other. The paper will open into a star shape with a handle attached.

17. Completed Magic Wand, shown open.

Party Favors

Prepare a Magic Wand for each guest. You can write each person's name on the handle. If you present the Magic Wands closed, guests will be amazed when you show them how to work the wand. On the other hand, your table will look more festive if you present the Magic Wand opened.

Lock

You can lock the Magic Wand. Cut one end of the strip to be about ¾" (2 cm) shorter than the other. Then you can fold up the longer end and slide it into the other end of the strip. Or attach a paper clip.

◣ COMPETITIONS

Competitions with origami can add a lot of entertainment at parties and other events. Here are some ideas.

Plane contests can be held indoors or outdoors. Contestants construct their own paper airplanes. Later they fly them for record distance or longest time aloft. All participants can fly the same kind of airplane or make up their own designs.

For a frog jumping contest players flip origami frogs into a bowl. Determine rules about how far away the jumps start, how many tries each person gets, and the size of the frogs. Read "The Celebrated Frog of Calaveras County" by Mark Twain for more ideas.

For a mask parade, set up a table with boxes filled with paper, glue, and many add-ons, such as markers, feathers, and leaves. Allow plenty of time for everyone to create fancy masks before having a parade with judging of the best, the funniest, the most original, and other categories.

After an origami model is taught to a group, let everyone try to recreate it. The three people who finish first are the winners. Or after everybody has folded a model, they unfold the paper flat and color the different triangles and other geometric shapes that appear. Young children can be challenged to identify the shapes.

Many origamis can be lined up for use in counting games.

People stand in pairs, opposite each other. Each pair is to fold a certain origami together but with each person using only one hand. The pair who completes the model first is the winner.

Pin an origami model to the back of a person, who then has to ask questions of the other people to find out what it is.

Some of these contests proved hilarious when they were held at conferences of paperfolders.

ACKNOWLEDGEMENTS

I owe a debt of gratitude to many friends in the international origami community who, over many years, have always been ready to share their interest in origami. I wish I could name everyone, but regret that is impossible. I would like to thank those who have patiently participated in the time-consuming task of testing the directions: Heather and Julia Anderson, John Andrisan, Jackie Booth, Sharon Brengel, Jim Cowling, V'Ann Cornelius, Charles de Stefano, Ed Epps, Steve Hecht, Judy Jaskowiak, Cath Kachur, Zoe Lehman, Dane Petersen, Nancy Petersen, Lisa and Mark Saliers, Yvonne Perez-Collins, Arlene Pollock, Shoshana Resnikoff, David and Michael Sanchez, Arnold Tubis, members of Origami San Diego, and, of course, my grandchildren, Tyler and Yolanda Anyon; Erin Hook; Dennis and Janet Temko; David, Perri, and Rachel Temko.